# SCREEN-FREE FUN

Published in 2021 by The School of Life
First published in the USA in 2021
70 Marchmont Street, London WC1N 1AB

Copyright © The School of Life 2021

Typeset by Jack Smyth
Printed in Latvia by Livonia Print

A proportion of this book has appeared online at www.theschooloflife.com/thebookoflife

Every effort has been made to contact the copyright holders of the material reproduced in this book. If any have been inadvertently overlooked, the publisher will be pleased to make restitution at the earliest opportunity.

The School of Life is a resource for helping us understand ourselves, for improving our relationships, our careers and our social lives – as well as for helping us find calm and get more out of our leisure hours. We do this through creating films, workshops, books, apps and gifts.

www.theschooloflife.com

ISBN 978-1-912891-57-3

10 9 8 7 6 5 4 3 2 1

MIX
Paper from
responsible sources
FSC® C002795

# SCREEN-FREE

# FUN

The School of Life

# CONTENTS

# INTRODUCTION

These days, our lives are filled with screens. They come in all shapes and sizes: some as large as a sports pitch; some small enough to fit on your wrist. There are screens at bus stops and on billboards; screens on the backs of aeroplane seats and the front of shops; screens in pockets, handbags, rucksacks, and everywhere else in between. If you look up from this book right now, you might be able to spot one, maybe sat in the corner of your living room, lying on the kitchen table, or held in the hands of someone in your family. On average, someone your age spends between five and seven hours a day looking at some form of screen. And adults are even worse, spending between eleven and thirteen hours with their screens.

Why do we all like screens so much? The answer is simple: we use screens to protect ourselves from one of life's least pleasant sensations: boredom. We're all familiar with the feeling. It might come when we're stuck inside on a Sunday afternoon, listening to the rain hammering on the roof. Or on a long car journey down the motorway, staring glumly out the window. When nothing seems to be happening, no one else is around to play with, and we can't think of anything better to do, we reach for a screen. We get bored because our minds are naturally, constantly, endlessly curious. Our minds, like our bellies, have big appetites.

Just like hunger is a signal sent by your stomach that it needs food, boredom is a signal from your mind telling you it needs something to occupy it: a new idea, sensation, experience or activity. That doesn't have to come from watching videos or messing around with apps. It can come from learning new facts, or practising a skill, or creating a piece of art. So long as we're prepared to be imaginative, there are infinite possibilities for banishing boredom and having fun, even when we're stuck indoors.

In this book, you'll find 80 alternatives to using a screen. They are activities: some fascinating, some helpful, and some very silly. Rather than scroll or tap, you'll be invited to draw, make, write, invent, dress up, hide, seek and discover. You won't need any special equipment; only the items from around your home. For some, you might need to recruit a brother, sister, friend or parent, but most you can do on your own. Some require you to do something fiddly and a little bit risky, like using scissors. For some you might need some supervision. But most require nothing but your imagination.

You can work through the activities in order, or pick one at random. You can do one to fill ten minutes, or a few to fill a whole afternoon. They might make you laugh, or scream, or pull a face, but we guarantee you'll never be bored.

# INDOOR ENTOMOLOGY

Some people get paid to look at bugs all day. They are called entomologists. They know that the closer you pay attention to things, the more interesting they become.

There are a surprising number of bugs living alongside you in your home. Here are a few different types.

See how many different types you find in the house, and make a note of your findings with a pen and paper.

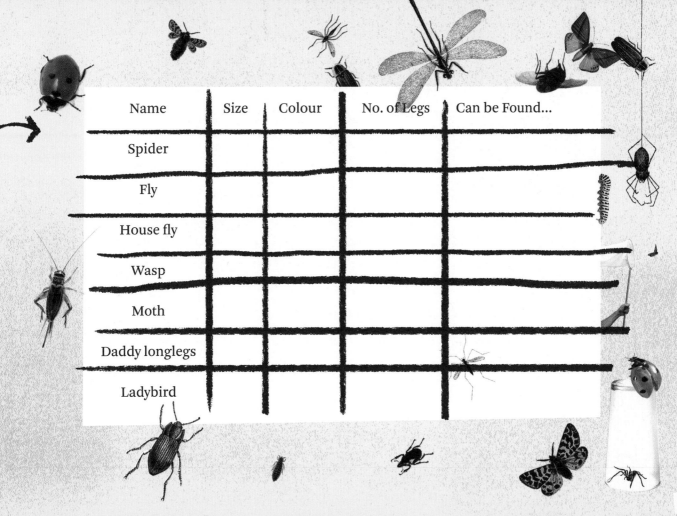

| Name | Size | Colour | No. of Legs | Can be Found... |
|---|---|---|---|---|
| Spider | | | | |
| Fly | | | | |
| House fly | | | | |
| Wasp | | | | |
| Moth | | | | |
| Daddy longlegs | | | | |
| Ladybird | | | | |

# KNIGHT-IN-DINING-ARMOUR

Check with a grown-up before doing this activity.

In medieval times, knights would travel the country performing noble deeds. They often wore a suit of armour to protect them.

Make your own suit of armour using items you find in the kitchen.

→ Big pots and colanders make good helmets.

→ Baking trays make good breastplates.

→ Pans make good shields.

→ Wooden spoons make good swords.
(Don't use any dangerous items – like kitchen knives – and try not to start any fights with fellow knights.)

# NOT-SO-SUPER HEROES

Superheroes are imaginary characters who have special powers. These are usually useful abilities – like super strength, or invisibility – that they use to help people. But it might be more fun to imagine characters with useless abilities.

Make up your own hero – except instead of having a useful superpower, they should be as useless as possible.

Cabbage Man
*Power*: Smells like cabbage
*Uses*: Spoiling dinner parties

Slightly-See-Through Woman
*Power*: Turning invisible (but only a bit)
*Uses*: Being able to sit in front of the TV and have people look through

13

# WINDOW STAKEOUT

Detectives are very good at coping with boredom. They need to be patient (good at waiting) and observant (good at watching).

When they're investigating a case, they'll sometimes have a stakeout – which means they'll spend a long time watching a person or building and keeping notes about what happens.

Test your detective skills by sitting by the window for half an hour with a pen and paper. Keep detective-type notes about anything that happens. For example:

**11:12:** Next-door's cat jumps on top of the bins.

**11:14:** A woman with a pram goes past.

**11:17:** A man gets out of a big white van and ties his shoelace.

**11:18:** Next-door's cat gets off the bin.

**11:22:** It starts raining.

**11:25:** The postman turns up and delivers some letters.

**11:26:** The postman stops to stroke next-door's cat.

# POO EULOGY

Speeches tend to be quite boring. They involve lots of talking about quite dull topics and mostly go on far too long.

When someone dies, their loved ones will write a eulogy – a speech that celebrates their good qualities and expresses sadness that they have gone.

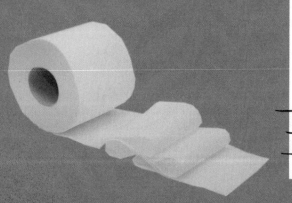

Write a eulogy of your own – except instead of writing about someone who has died, write about the last poo you had.
Try to work in some poo-based puns.

→ 'Dearly pooloved, we are gathered here today...'
→ 'Flushed before their time...'
→ 'Gases-to-gases, flush-to-flush...'

# MY UTOPIA

In most spaces, grown-ups, not children, make the rules. Your parents make the rules in your house, your teachers make the rules at school. But if you had a country of your own, just imagine the rules you could make up...

A utopia is a 'perfect' society – one where all the rules have been designed to ensure the greatest amount of happiness for those who live there.

Build yourself a private utopia by throwing an old bedsheet over the kitchen table. What's inside is your utopia. Inside, you make the rules – ones that ensure the greatest amount of happiness for yourself (and anyone who comes to join you).

Write a list of laws that must be observed in your little country:

 Everyone has to call me Chief, King/Queen or Boss.

 The only food allowed is sweets.

 You have to whisper.

You have to wear mismatched socks.

# STILL LIFE

Artists usually paint pictures of people, or nice views. But some artists paint everyday objects – like bowls of fruit, or flowers, or objects they find around them.

Check with a grown-up before making a mess.

Make your own still-life picture. Gather together a few objects from around the house and then try to draw or paint them as accurately as you can.

Here are some selections of objects that we like:

➤ A can of soup, an orange, a lightbulb and a pencil.

➤ A toaster, a phone charger, a feather and a teaspoon.

# IMPRESS YOUR PARENTS

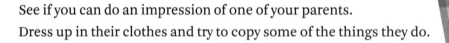

An impressionist is someone who copies someone else, imitating the way they look, sound and behave. Some very talented impressionists have become famous and made a lot of money.

See if you can do an impression of one of your parents.
Dress up in their clothes and try to copy some of the things they do.

→ How do they walk?

→ How do they sound?

→ What kinds of things do they say?

If you're feeling brave, you might want to show your impression to your parents. You might discover that one finds it funnier than the other.

# RUDE WORDS

Dictionaries can look quite boring. But they're more interesting than they look. They give you the meaning of all sorts of different words – even the rude ones.

If you have a dictionary somewhere in the house, have a look through and try to find the silliest, strangest, rudest words you can find.

Here are some good ones we found:

FLIBBERTIGIBBET

COLLYWOBBLES

BUMFUZZLE

→ bumfuzzle (v.) – confused
→ collywobbles (n.) – a strange feeling in your stomach
→ flibbertigibbet (n.) – a silly, talkative person

Afterwards you could try using them in conversation to impress your friends and family with your vast (and naughty) vocabulary.

# NEWSTACHES

The Walrus

People in newspapers are usually very serious – or at least trying to appear so. But this is mostly an act: deep down, they're just as silly and ridiculous as you sometimes are. They might be the leader of a political party or the head of a company, but they probably still spill drinks on themselves, or trip over their shoelaces.

The Goatee

It's good to remind yourself of this by making people in newspapers look as silly on the outside as they are inside. To do so, find an old newspaper and a black pen. Give everyone in the newspaper a moustache. Try to use a different style for every moustache. Here are a few examples…

The Handlebar

# FECKLESS NECKLACE

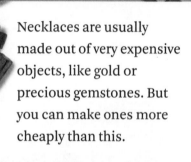

Necklaces are usually made out of very expensive objects, like gold or precious gemstones. But you can make ones more cheaply than this.

If you have a piece of string, try making a necklace out of small objects you find around the house. We recommend using:

→ Buttons
→ Paper clips
→ Keys
→ Uncooked pasta pieces
→ Picture hooks
→ Pen lids with holes in the top

# RACING RAINDROPS

Racing raindrops is a sport that, sadly, hasn't yet become as popular as football. But maybe it will one day.

Sit by a window and watch the raindrops rolling down. Can you guess which droplet will reach the bottom first? Keep practising – see if your skills develop.

If you have a friend or sibling with you, you could both try to guess – see which one of you wins the race.

Start to look out for rainy days and celebrate them when they arrive.

# INTERVIEW YOUR GRANDMOTHER

Grown-ups tend to be very busy, but older grown-ups – like your grandmother, for example – are usually retired and may have more time on their hands.

Why not write your grandmother* a letter? If you ask the right questions, you'll realise she's much more fascinating than you might have first thought.

*or another elderly person you know

You could start by asking how she is, then doing a little investigation to discover more about her. She probably has lots of interesting things to tell you.

> Ask her what her own childhood was like.
> Ask her what your mum or dad was like when they were little.
> Ask her what she does now she's retired.
> Ask her how she met your grandfather.
> Ask her whether she remembers witnessing an important event from history.

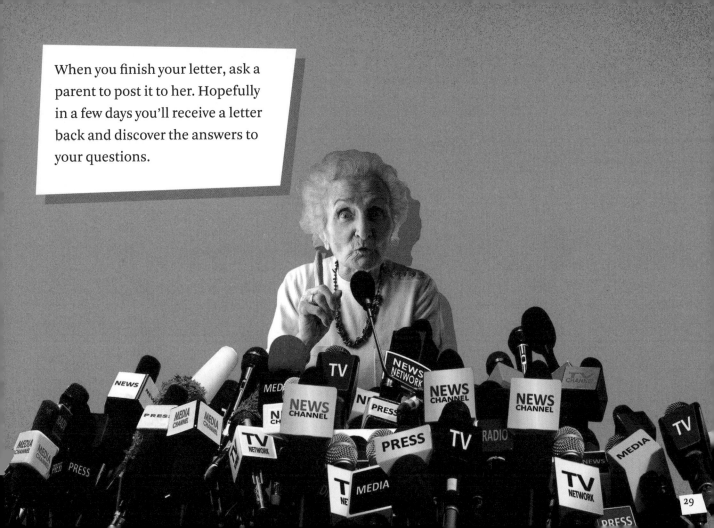

When you finish your letter, ask a parent to post it to her. Hopefully in a few days you'll receive a letter back and discover the answers to your questions.

# PAINT LIKE PICASSO

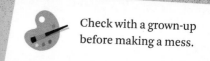

Check with a grown-up before making a mess.

Pablo Picasso was a famous artist from Spain. He didn't try to paint things exactly as they looked in real life (he found this quite boring). Instead, he liked to experiment by painting them in as many different ways as he could think of.

Pick a person or object – maybe one of your parents or siblings, or a piece of furniture in your room.
Try to think of different ways you can draw them/it.

Can you draw them/it using only one colour?
Can you draw them/it out of shapes (like cubes, circles or triangles)?
Can you draw them in the weirdest way you can think of?

# BOTTLE INSTRUMENT

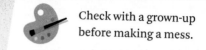 Check with a grown-up before making a mess.

Musical instruments are often very tempting to play with. They're also very expensive (and harder to use than they look), which means people are always telling you not to touch them. But luckily, you can make music even if you don't have a guitar or a cello to hand.

Find some empty bottles (the more you have the better). Fill them with water to differing levels (mostly full, quite full, halfway full, quite empty, mostly empty) and arrange them in order.

You can now make different notes by tapping each bottle with a spoon or blowing over the tops of them. See if you can play a song someone else can recognise. If things are going well, start a water bottle band. Find yourself a good name.If things are going really well, fill bottles with different sorts of liquid. What happens to the sound when you fill a bottle with milk, or creamy soup? (Make sure you ask an adult before using a different liquid – and don't drink any afterwards!)

# MEDITATION

Our minds are always full of different thoughts, but we tend not to pay much attention to them. Some people, like Buddhists, use a technique called meditation to slow down and focus on what's happening in their minds.

Announce to your family that you're off to meditate for half an hour (some Buddhist monks meditate for 48 hours, but we don't recommend that yet).

→ Sit quietly in your room with your legs crossed and your eyes closed.

→ Try not to think about anything special (that's a bit odd in itself; normally, we're just living, not thinking about living), just focus on the contents of your mind.

→ Feel your breath going in and out, how your skin feels against the floor, and let any background noise fade away.

→ Start to notice what you might be a bit anxious about; what might have upset you, and what you might be really looking forward to (what's beautiful and exciting).

Have a pad of paper and a pen near you and jot down things that are interesting. You might learn all sorts of new things about yourself by paying close attention to the traffic in your own head.

# STEERING BLIND

 Be careful never to steer them into anything or near the stairs!

As soon as you shut your eyes, the world becomes a very different place. When you can't see anything, you have to rely on your other senses – particularly touch, sounds, and the memory of the two – to move around. The smallest journey around a room starts to be an adventure, full of danger and a kind of excitement too.

Get a friend to play this game with you. Begin by asking them to lock their eyes firmly shut (make them promise they won't look until you say so). Then steer them around the room, saying: Forwards, Backwards, Left, Right – and add in Slower and Faster.

The job is to get them to avoid colliding with anything. At first, they'll probably move very slowly and be a bit scared. But with time, they'll get more confident. You might steer them around the whole of the ground floor without them bumping into everything.

# GOOD NEWS

Most of the news is either dull, confusing or miserable (and sometimes all three at once). This is because it's usually about things that have gone wrong – like floods, or wars.

But news that focuses only on what's wrong is ridiculous, given how much goes right every day.

Here is a chance for you to redraw the balance. Using a pen and paper, make your own newspaper. Only this time, you choose the headlines. Instead of recording things that have gone wrong, your newspaper should focus on things that have gone right. Start with the life around you.

**YOUNG GIRL LEARNS TO TIE SHOELACES**

**BOY GETS PRETTY GOOD MARK ON SCIENCE HOMEWORK**

**DAD LEARNS NOT TO SWEAR SO MUCH WHEN HE LOSES KEYS**

Then think about your country. It has problems, of course, but what's going pretty well in it? Here are some ideas:

**ELECTRICITY GRID LIGHTS UP EVERYONE'S HOUSE YET AGAIN!**

**BIGGEST POOS GET BEAUTIFULLY SWEPT INTO THE DRAINAGE SYSTEM AND TURNED INTO CLEAN WASTE**

**45 DIFFERENT KINDS OF BREAD AVAILABLE IN AVERAGE SUPERMARKET!**

It's good to develop the art of reminding yourself of things that are going well in life. Any old idiot can find the bad news; only really clever people are good at hunting out, and keeping in mind, the good news.

# CHANGE YOUR VIEW

The view out of your bedroom window probably isn't all that exciting – if you even have one at all.

Take a big sheet of paper and some colouring pencils. Draw yourself a more interesting view. Use your imagination. Maybe your bedroom looks out on an old castle, or a futuristic city, or an underwater seascape.

When you're finished, stick the view on your bedroom wall with some Sticky Putty or Blu-Tack.

# CUT-UP TECHNIQUE

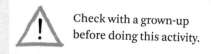

!  Check with a grown-up before doing this activity.

During the last century, some famous experimental writers – like Tristan Tzara and William Burroughs – began making up poems by cutting out words or sentences from newspapers or magazines and arranging them to make new sentences. They called this 'cut-up technique'.

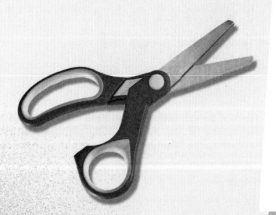

Find an old newspaper. With some scissors, cut out a number of words or phrases. Once you've done so, jumble up all the clippings on a table (or in a hat, if you can find one).

Then pick different clippings at random and arrange them into sentences. Don't worry if they don't make sense – it's more important that they sound unusual or exciting.

THOUSANDS of motorists will

end up in the ocean

says chancellor

scattering nasturtiums and tagetes

A man has been charged with

heat the oven to 210C

scientists warn

DOGS ARE ABLE TO

# CLEANING PIONEER

 Check with a grown-up before doing this activity.

There are few things more boring than chores – and few chores more boring than cleaning. One way to make things more interesting is by becoming a cleaning pioneer.

A pioneer is the first person in history to do a particular thing – like climb a certain mountain, or visit an uninhabited island. Pioneers are celebrated for daring to achieve things no other person has done before them.

Find a hidden and neglected spot in your house that has rarely – if ever – been cleaned before, and give it a brush, dust or wipe. This might be:

→ The ceiling of the wardrobe.
→ The gap behind the toilet.
→ The space behind a radiator.
→ The wall behind a painting or photograph.

You'll not only be doing something helpful (that your family will be grateful for) – you'll be pioneering a new form of cleaning in the process.

# BECOME AN ANIMAL

Many adults tend to make a huge deal about the difference between animals and humans, but in many ways there's really not such a gap.

Choose an animal you like (maybe you have a favourite). Spend the day pretending to be this animal. See if you can:

→ <u>Dress up like an animal</u>: For example, a tortoise might wear a laundry basket on its back; a bear might wear a big furry coat.

→ <u>Walk like an animal</u>: An elephant walks very slowly on all fours (stomping its feet); a chicken walks quickly while bobbing its head and flapping.

→ <u>Speak like an animal</u>: A lion roars and growls; a mouse squeaks; a kookaburra laughs.

→ <u>Act like an animal</u>: Birds spend the day gathering twigs to make nests; hamsters stuff food in their cheeks for safekeeping; ducks like eating bread and splashing about in water.

To make it a game, keep up your act in front of your family, agreeing to stop only when they correctly guess what animal you are or when 12 hours have gone by.

# CLOUD WATCHING

Have you ever noticed that, on bright clear days, a cloud sometimes looks like something else? Like a face, an object or an animal?

Lie on your back and look up at the clouds. See how many different things you can spot:

→ A guitar?
→ A bungalow?
→ A sausage dog?

→ Two men fighting?
→ A sailboat?
→ A brain?

# BORED STIFF

On particularly dull days, we might say that we're feeling 'bored stiff' – as though we're so bored that we've turned to stone. Instead of fighting this feeling, why not embrace it by turning it into a game?

Lie on the floor with your eyes closed. Be completely still, keeping your body as rigid as possible. Try to lie like this for five minutes (which will feel closer to five years).

Use the time to think about all the things you'd miss doing if you really had been turned to stone – like running across the grass in your bare feet, playing with a favourite old toy, or picking the fluff out of your belly button.

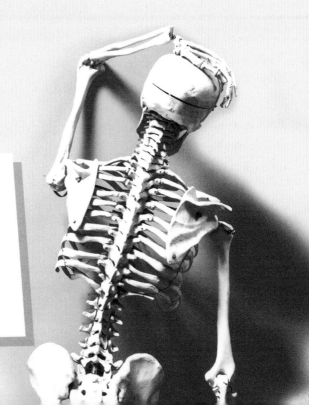

When you get up, you should feel newly excited about all the different ways you might spend the rest of the day. Nothing's that boring when compared to being as stiff as a stone!

# YOUR OWN ORCHARD

Check with a grown-up before making a mess.

If you think about it, it's incredible that such large things in nature – like trees – start their lives as such small objects – like seeds.

→ The next time you have an apple, instead of throwing the core away, split it open and take out the apple seeds. Leave them to dry on a paper towel for a day or so.

→ Find a small pot and fill it with soil (you could try using any soil, but special seed-starting soil works best). Make a few small holes in the soil with your little finger and drop one seed into each hole, covering the top with more soil.

→ Keep the pot somewhere warm and sunny, watering it every couple of days. Not every seed will grow into a tree, but with any luck, within a month or two, you should be able to see shoots beginning to grow.

Eventually you'll need to replant them outside so they can grow into trees. Make sure you ask your parents before doing so!

# COMBINING FLAVOURS

Ask a grown-up for help with this activity.

People who cook tend to have strict ideas of what 'goes' with what: mustard is good with steak, but not so good with chocolate. Mayonnaise goes well with tuna, but is a bit weird with carrots...

Some of these rules are wise enough, but what about trying deliberately to break them in a search for some of the strangest, most surprising and sometimes most disgusting flavour combinations imaginable?

In your kitchen, set out to mix some unlikely ingredients:

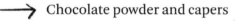 Chocolate powder and capers    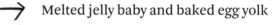 Melted jelly baby and baked egg yolk

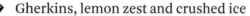 Gherkins, lemon zest and crushed ice     Horseradish and cottage cheese

Prepare a few of these surprising 'dishes' for other members of your family (get a grown-up to help you if you need to do anything a bit dangerous, like cutting up vegetables or using the oven) and ask them to guess what they are eating. Reassure them that there's nothing dangerous in the mix. Lastly, do the washing-up!

# LIFE PREDICTIONS

A common thought when you're stuck inside with nothing to do is 'at least I won't feel like this when I'm older'. Sadly, this probably won't be the case – grown-ups frequently get bored too – but it is interesting to think about the future.

Make some predictions about how your life will turn out when you're older. What will you do for a job? What sort of house will you live in? Will you be married? If so, what sort of person might you be married to?

I will have a job as a train driver.

I will live in a big mansion with a pool in Los Angeles.

I will be married to my brother's friend Darren.

I will have six children – three boys and three girls – and a black sheepdog called Remington.

Making predictions will help you start to think about the kind of life you want to lead, and what you might need to start doing in order to achieve it.

When you're finished, put your predictions in an envelope and keep it somewhere very safe, like inside an old book or beneath a floorboard. Then, wait a while – say ten or twenty years – before taking it out again. It will be very interesting to see what you got wrong, or right.

# LEAF PRESSING

It's a little sad to think that leaves are often at their most beautiful in autumn – just as they're dying and falling off the trees.

Gather up some leaves that you find outside (it's best to do this in autumn, when there are more on the ground).

When you're back inside, find the biggest, thickest book you can find. Put the leaves between the pages in the middle. Then close the book and pile as many more as you can on top of it.

Leave it for about a week and you'll have a memento of autumn, perfectly preserved.

# UNIQUE PERSPECTIVES

One of the reasons we get bored when we're at home is because the environment has become over-familiar. We're used to looking at the exact same things in the same way – our bedroom ceiling, our living room wall – over and over. Our eyes – and minds – are tired of sameness.

To make things more interesting, what we need is a different perspective to see old things in a new way. Try to find a vantage point that allows you to look at things differently. How does the room look when you are:

→ **Lying upside down on the sofa?**

→ **Rolled up inside the carpet?**

→ **Crouching underneath a table?**

→ **Peering through a full glass of water?**

The world is almost never boring; we're just looking at it from a boring angle.

# CONCOCTING CONSTELLATIONS

On certain clear nights, you can look up and see lots of stars. People have been doing this for thousands of years. They learned to recognise particular stars by drawing patterns between them – patterns that looked like objects ('the plough'), animals ('the ram') or people ('Orion, the hunter').

Take a piece of paper and draw the pattern of stars in the night sky (either by copying a photograph you've taken, or by trying to copy the sky as you see it outside your window). Then, make your own constellations by 'joining the dots'.

See if you can make your patterns look like particular people, animals or objects.

# MEMORY CAPSULE

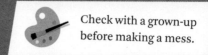

Check with a grown-up before making a mess.

Memory is a surprisingly fickle thing. You probably won't remember what you did today in a month's time. In a year's time, you probably won't remember most of what you did this month... and in ten years' time, you probably won't remember anything that happened this year. It therefore helps if you can keep a record.

First, find a sturdy container, like a biscuit tin or a shoebox. Then, start filling it up with objects that mean something to you at this point in your life. Things like:

- A painting you've done at school.
- A piece of homework you're proud of.
- A photo of you and your friends.

- An object you use as part of a favourite hobby, such as a bootlace (for football) or a shuttlecock (for badminton).

When you've filled the container, bury it somewhere in the garden (try not to dig up any plants or flowers). Then, when you're five or so years older, you can dig it up and rediscover the person you were at your current age.

# POEMEMORY

Memorising poems can be a useful skill – grown-ups tend to be very impressed if you can recite a poem from memory alone.

Here's one to get you started. It's by a very famous American poet called Emily Dickinson.

Read the poem a few times, then practise saying each line to yourself with your eyes closed until you have the whole thing committed to memory.

## I'M NOBODY! WHO ARE YOU?

I'm nobody! Who are you?
Are you nobody, too?
Then there's a pair of us – don't tell!
They'd banish us, you know.
How dreary to be somebody!
How public, like a frog
To tell your name the livelong day
To an admiring bog!

# RECEIPT TOP TRUMPS

A receipt is a record of a sale; you get given one whenever you pay for something in a shop. It records different information about the sale – the amount of money you paid, as well as the date and the time of day you bought the item. You probably have a few receipts lying about in your home.

Gather together as many different receipts you can find (pockets, bags and drawers are a good place to look). Then, with a friend or family member, shuffle the receipts and deal them between the two of you. You can then play a game of 'receipt Top Trumps'.

→ Players take it in turns to say either the amount, date or time they have on their receipt.

→ The other player compares this to the amount, date or time they have on their own receipt.

→ Whichever player has the highest amount or the most recent date or time 'wins'.

→ The losing player gives their receipt to the winning player.

Keep playing until one player has all the receipts.

# SURPRISING ENTERPRISE

An entrepreneur is someone who sets up an entirely new kind of business – a company that does or makes something that no one else has thought of doing or making before.

Most entrepreneurs start by identifying a common problem people have, and then inventing a product or service that can solve this problem.

Think up some problems you encounter in your day-to-day life, then try to imagine a product or service that could help.

| PROBLEM | SOLUTION |
| --- | --- |
| I can't reach the top shelf of the cupboard in the kitchen. | Product: A miniature step-ladder for kids |
| The cat isn't allowed outside, but needs to get exercise. | Product: A big hamster wheel for cats |
| I can't go and play in the park because it's raining. | Service: A mobile park – a truck with grass and play equipment inside that travels around to different houses for children to play in on rainy days |

Make a list of 10 big problems you can see in your life and the lives of those around you. Now dream up some business solutions.

# RUDE WORDSEARCH

When people are bored they will sometimes do puzzles – like crosswords or wordsearches – as a way of passing the time. But it can be even more absorbing to create puzzles of your own – especially if you get to be a bit rude when doing it.

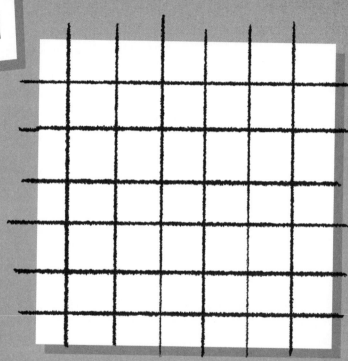

First, draw an empty grid on a piece of paper using a pencil and a ruler.

Next, write in some words vertically, horizontally or diagonally. (We think rude ones work best.)

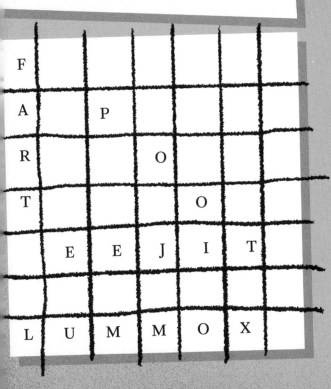

| F |   |   |   |   |   |
|---|---|---|---|---|---|
| A |   | P |   |   |   |
| R |   |   | O |   |   |
| T |   |   |   | O |   |
|   | E | E | J | I | T |
| L | U | M | M | O | X |

Finally, fill in the empty spaces on the grid with some randomly chosen letters.

| F | T | Y | U | C | V | H |
|---|---|---|---|---|---|---|
| A | W | P | G | V | W | S |
| R | Y | Z | O | X | B | V |
| T | C | K | F | O | F | T |
| L | E | E | J | I | T | N |
| F | G | A | Q | Y | M | I |
| L | U | M | M | O | X | P |

You now have a wordsearch ready to go. Give it to a friend or someone in their family to complete (telling them it helps to be in an impolite frame of mind).

# BODY KNOWLEDGE

Your body probably doesn't seem very interesting any more. After all, the two of you do everything together. You're pretty used to each other by now. But there's a lot you probably still don't know. For example, could you tell someone exactly:

→ How many teeth you have?
→ How long your earlobes are?
→ How wide your belly button is?
→ How many lines you have on your palms?

Find out, using rulers and mirrors to help you. Keep a record of your results – perhaps one you could add to in future to see what might have changed.

# PENNY FINDERS

Grown-ups spend a lot of time thinking about money – how much of it they're earning, what they're spending it on, and how much of it they still have left. So it's surprising how much of it they lose around the house (particularly pennies).

Search the house and see how much of it you can collect. Try looking:

→ Between the cushions of the sofa.
→ Under the carpet.
→ In coat pockets.
→ Below the bookcase.

# FEED THE BIRDS

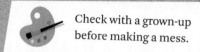

Check with a grown-up before making a mess.

People who pass the time by watching birds are called birdwatchers. Some birdwatchers travel great distances and wait huge lengths of time in order to spot particular varieties. But you can become a birdwatcher without even leaving your garden.

The best way to attract birds to your garden is by making a bird feeder.

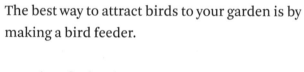

→ First, find a pine cone.

→ Then mix together some butter with other small items of food in a bowl – like seeds, berries, raisins and grated cheese.

→ Spread the mixture on the pine cone and tie it with string to a tree outside your window.

→ Then wait and see which birds come to visit your feeder.

If you have a book of birds, you can learn  to recognise the different types.

# NEW GODS

Throughout history, people have believed in a god – and sometimes more than one. The ancient Greeks, for example, had hundreds: a god of love, and one of war; a god of wine, and a god of grain; a god of the sea, and of fire, and of the dead.

Invent your own god. Try to answer the following questions:

→ How were they created?
→ Are they the god of anything in particular?
→ What powers do they have?
→ How would you worship them?
→ What are their followers called?

If you're particularly proud of your creation, you can try making a shrine to them in your bedroom – a little space to honour and pray to them. Decorate it with candles, drawings and precious things you find around the house.

# INVENT A LANGUAGE

We're still not quite sure how different languages evolve. But some people have invented languages – usually as a way of communicating in secret. One example of an invented code language is Pig Latin, where the first letter of each word is moved to the end with the suffix '-ay'.

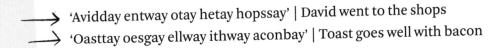

'Avidday entway otay hetay hopssay' | David went to the shops

'Oasttay oesgay ellway ithway aconbay' | Toast goes well with bacon

Make up your own coded language. Come up with a simple rule that you can use to disguise the words you're saying. Maybe one where every vowel sound is pronounced the same? Or where all the syllables are reversed?

You can then teach your language to a trusted friend or sibling so the two of you can communicate in secret.

# STAND AND DELIVER

A highwayman was a kind of robber who lived in the 1700s. They wore disguises and carried masks. They would wait by the roadside at night and surprise travellers, holding them at gunpoint until they handed over their money and valuables.

You can try being a highwayman at home. Make yourself a disguise (an eye mask or an old tea towel will do), find a weapon (wooden spoon or cardboard tube) , and lie in wait in a room off the corridor in your house. When a member of your family comes along, stop them and make them:

a) give you any valuables they have.

b) ask them to tell you in detail why you shouldn't kill them.

Let them pass if they do well (and give them back their valuables).

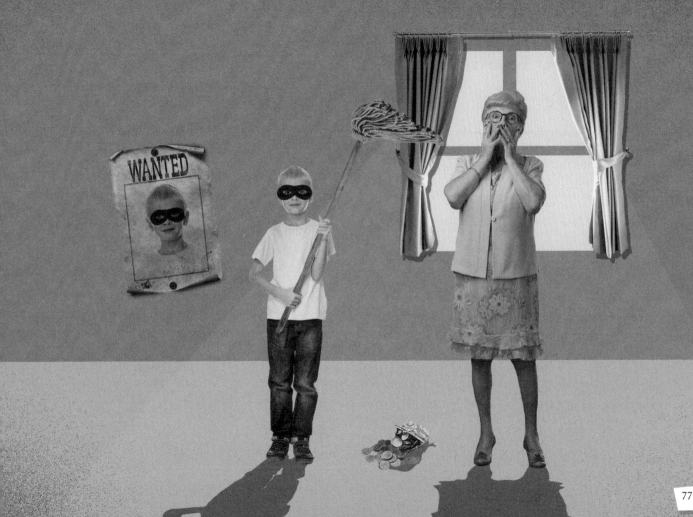

# EGG FAMILY

 Ask a grown-up for help with this activity.

Parents are rather keen on family portraits – you've probably been made to sit for a group photograph (and maybe more than one). You can make a different kind of family portrait.

First, find some eggs – one for each member of your family. You might want to get a grown-up to hard-boil them for you to make things easier.

Then, using pens (or ideally some paints and a brush), decorate the eggs to look like members of your family.

Display them in eggcups (if you have them) and give them to your parents as a present.

# DRESSING UP, UP AND UP

Most of the time we get told what to wear, although sometimes we're allowed to dress up for fun by putting on costumes. But there are different types of fun you can have by dressing up.

See how many different items of clothing you can put on at once.

→ How many pairs of socks and underwear?
→ How many T-shirts and jumpers?
→ How many pairs of trousers?
→ How many hats?

To make a game of it, have a race with a friend or sibling, timing each other to see how many different items you can put on in 30 seconds, or seeing who can be the first to put on 20 different items.

# PRECIOUS SUITCASE

You probably have a lot of different possessions – far too many to fit in a single bag, cupboard, or even room. But trying to think what you really, really need is a useful exercise.

Find an empty suitcase. Pack it full of all your most precious possessions – the clothes, toys, books, gadgets, photographs and other items that you simply couldn't do without if, for example, you had to leave home forever.

You can only pack what fits in the suitcase, which means you'll have to make some decisions about what items you simply have to have and which items you'll have to leave behind.

Doing this might help you work out what is most important to you.

# DRAWPRECIATION

When we concentrate very hard on something, we can come to appreciate it in a whole new way: it can seem amazing and beautiful. One way of paying close attention to something is to draw it.

Find a pencil and some paper and a family member who is willing to be very patient and sit quietly next to you. Then try to draw one of their hands.

Try to capture as much detail as possible – the shadows between the fingers, the wrinkles on the knuckles, the shape of the veins underneath the skin.

Not only will you be developing your drawing skills, you'll be paying someone the compliment of devoting a lot of time and attention to them.

# RECIPE FOR DISASTER

A recipe tells you the ingredients and method for making a meal. Finding the recipe for a really good meal takes a lot of time and practice, neither of which is particularly fun.

Write your own recipe, except rather than trying to make a dish someone might want to eat, try to imagine the most off-putting meal possible using every disgusting ingredient you can think of.

1. Mix together 200g of soil with 200g of cornflakes.
2. Add a squirt of toothpaste.
3. Add a pinch of dandruff and a drop of spit.
4. Put in two teaspoonfuls of cod liver oil.
5. Add one mashed mud cake and half a pint of milk.
6. Put it in the oven at gas mark 6 for 1 hour.
7. Add toenail clippings to serve.

We don't recommend trying to actually make your meals – the goal should be to think up something so disgusting just reading the recipe is enough to make you gag.

# RECIPES

# MY CHIMERA

 Check with a grown-up before doing this activity.

Animals come in lots of shapes and sizes – some of them very strange indeed. If you use your imagination, you can come up with an animal that is even stranger than one that already exists. A chimera is a mythical beast that is made up from parts of other animals.

You could have a chimera with the head of a canary, the body of a horse, the feet of a panther and the tail of a fish. Or one with the head of a monkey, the horns of a goat, the body of a walrus and the tail of a peacock. Make up a chimera of your own, either by using your imagination and drawing one, or by cutting out parts of different animals from nature magazines and sticking them together on a piece of paper.

# GRUE-SEUM

Museums are collections of interesting things – whether that be old paintings, or fossils, or stuffed animals, or stamps, or paper clips, or bowler hats (all of these are real museums you can visit).

Why not try making your own museum by collecting something you find a lot of around the house? Something a bit unusual, or a little bit disgusting.
You could set up:

→ The Museum of Fluff
→ The Museum of Lost Socks
→ The Museum of Plughole Hair
→ The Museum of Dead Flies
→ The Museum of Toenail Clippings
→ The Museum of Bogeys

You can set up the museum in your bedroom, displaying your collection on tables or desks and charging members of your family a small amount to visit.

# NEW WORDS

There are an awful lot of words – nearly 200,000 in the English language alone. It is therefore surprising to think that there are so many things for which no word exists, particularly certain feelings or sensations.

When someone invents a brand new word for something, it's called a neologism (or sometimes a coinage). Some people have made quite a few neologisms – the playwright Shakespeare came up with around 2,000 of them!

Invent some words that can describe the following feelings and sensations:

→ The feeling when you've hurt yourself rather badly but are doing your best not to show your friends how much pain you're in.

→ The sensation when you put cold hands into hot water and for a moment the water feels icily cold.

→ The feeling when you dislike someone at school but pretend not to in order to fit in.

→ The sensation when you can tell that someone is standing behind you without looking.

→ The feeling when you're embarrassed watching someone else do something embarrassing (even though you don't really have a reason to be embarrassed).

Once you've done this, think about whether there are any other feelings or sensations you've experienced that don't have a name and come up with a word that might fit. You could also write these new words down somewhere to start a dictionary of brand new words.

# Menu

## Starters

CHOCOLATE PUDDING

ICE CREAM

## Main Course

SALAD

SOUP

## Dessert

BURGER & CHIPS

PIZZA

# BACK TO FRONT

Things are a bit more interesting back to front – have you ever watched a film in reverse, for example?

→ Dressing backwards (wearing your shirt, jeans and socks back to front).
→ Walking backwards.
→ Eating backwards (starting with pudding before the main course).
→ Speaking backwards (rearranging sentences back to front, e.g. 'Charlotte is name my, hi').
→ Writing backwards.

If you're feeling ambitious, you could have an entire 'back to front' day – having chicken pie and watching TV in the morning, and eating cornflakes and doing some colouring-in in the evening. You could get your family to join in.

# INTRIGUING OPENERS

Writing stories can be hard, especially if you can't think of an idea to write about. But sometimes all you need to get your imagination started is a good opening line.

Write some short stories that begin with the following opening lines:

→ On my tenth birthday, my parents surprised me with the news that I wasn't born on Planet Earth after all...

→ When I heard the bell ringing in the middle of the night and opened the door, never in a million years would I have guessed who'd be standing on the doorstep...

→ It was a sunny Saturday morning when my brother was kidnapped...

→ The first thing you should know about vampire school is that you aren't allowed to drink blood during lessons...

→ I sailed to the deserted island in search of treasure, but ended up finding something quite different...

On my tenth birthday, my parents surprised me with the news that I wasn't born on Planet Earth after all...

IT WAS A SUNNY SATURDAY MORNING WHEN MY BROTHER WAS KIDNAPPED...

When I I heard the bell ringing in the middle of the night, and opened the door, never in a million years would I have guessed who'd be standing on the doorstep...

I SAILED TO THE DESERTED ISLAND IN SEARCH OF TREASURE, BUT ENDED UP FINDING SOMETHING QUITE DIFFERENT...

# VOLUMINOUS VOCABULARY

A *sesquipedalian* is someone who knows a lot of different long words and uses them as often as possible.

Find a dictionary, open it at random, and choose a word – the longer and more complex the better. Memorise the meaning and practise the pronunciation.

Then, spend the rest of the day trying to use the word as often as you can. Drop it into conversation with your parents, siblings and friends.

To make it more challenging, memorise more words. See how many different new words you can learn and use in conversation to impress those you're speaking to. You'll be a sesquipedalian in no time!

# THE ENTHUSIASTIC SERVANT GAME

Doing what people want you to do is normally very boring, especially when your parents have chores in mind for you. But once you turn good behaviour into a game, it can get a lot more fun. Declare to one of your parents that you're going to be their 'servant' for a day. That means you will do whatever they want you to do. You might:

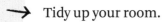

- Tidy up your room.
- Make them breakfast in bed.
- Fetch them something from the shops.
- Help them move a piece of furniture.

The rule is that you're not allowed to moan, you have to smile a lot and you have to seem genuinely enthusiastic. And your master has to have a list of things for you to do.

The good thing about being a servant is that the 'masters' are probably going to be quite nice to you – and that can be fun for everyone. Turn necessity into the best of all games!

# THE STORY OF AN OBJECT

Stories are usually written from the perspective of people. But, if you use your imagination, you might think about writing the stories of other things – including ones that aren't actually alive.

Pick an object you find around the house. Then take a pen and paper and write a story from the perspective of that object. Think about the kinds of things that have happened to it throughout its life, and try to imagine the thoughts and feelings it might have if it were somehow alive.

→ Maybe there's a spare sock in the dryer that feels lonely without its missing twin.

→ Maybe there's a mug that feels insecure because it has a chip in its handle.

→ Maybe there's a penny that has had a fascinating life – spending time in the pocket of a pop star, and the purse of a famous athlete – before ending up under your sofa.

# TASTE TESTER

 Ask a grown-up for help with this activity.

Most grown-up jobs don't sound very interesting, but one big exception is being a taste tester. Taste testers get paid to taste food to see whether it is flavoursome or not. There are ice-cream taste testers, biscuit taste testers, cake taste testers...

Practise your taste-testing skills by getting one of your parents to add a very small amount of a particular ingredient to different spoonfuls of a particular food, like custard or baked beans. Ingredients like:

→ Sugar
→ Salt
→ Lemon
→ Apple juice
→ Mustard
→ Soy sauce
→ Cocoa
→ Paprika
→ Saffron
→ Vanilla extract
→ Chili powder
→ Brown sauce

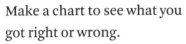

Make a chart to see what you got right or wrong.

Keep practising to hone your taste-testing skills.

# SUMMING IT UP

Here are four maths equations. You'll notice there's something missing.

| | | | | | | |
|---|---|---|---|---|---|---|
| (+/-) | 14 | 13 | 56 | 100 | 18 | = 53 |
| (x/÷) | 2 | 8 | 16 | 3 | 10 | = 30 |
| (+/-) | 77 | 12 | 1 | 11 | 6 | = 61 |
| (x /÷) | 101 | 8 | 3 | 4 | 11 | = 6666 |

We've taken away all the functions (the addition, subtraction, multiplication and division symbols). Add them back in, making sure the equations add up to the correct number. For each equation only use the symbols shown before it. You can use a calculator to help you (though not the one on a phone).

# PHILOSOPHERS' WORDSEARCH

| D | E | B | E | A | U | V | O | I | R |
|---|---|---|---|---|---|---|---|---|---|
| I | E | W | K | B | K | Z | L | R | O |
| D | J | S | O | C | R | A | T | E | S |
| E | I | A | C | M | L | H | U | M | E |
| R | S | R | Y | A | Y | V | G | C | R |
| O | K | T | D | R | R | A | W | L | S |
| T | J | R | V | X | Q | T | Q | H | Q |
| O | H | E | G | E | L | X | E | B | I |
| X | Y | T | J | C | A | M | U | S | M |
| G | P | N | F | P | A | S | C | A | L |

We've created a wordsearch using the names of some famous philosophers.

Can you find them all?

CAMUS
DE BEAUVOIR
DIDEROT
HEGEL
HUME
MARX
PASCAL
RAWLS
SARTRE
SOCRATES

# VOW OF SILENCE

Some religious people, like Christian or Buddhist monks, take what is called a vow of silence: going without speaking or making noise for a period of time as a way of honouring God. Some monks go months, years and even decades without saying a single word.

Take your own vow of silence. If you need to communicate with people, do so by using gestures, or by writing out words on a piece of paper or a whiteboard.

See how long you can be silent for. You can make it into a game by having a friend or sibling take a vow at the same time and seeing who can be silent for the longest. You might find that your parents are strangely grateful for your efforts...

# SOCK SLIDING

We often imagine people in ancient times walking around in sandals, or barefooted, but actually most of them wore socks, just like you. The ancient Greeks wore socks made out of animal hair; Roman socks were made from leather, while in the Middle Ages, noble lords and ladies wore fancy patterned socks to show how wealthy they were.

Nowadays we make socks out of more comfortable fabrics like cotton, which, as well as being warm, also make them excellent for sliding about on wooden or tiled floors.

Put on a pair of socks and find a polished bit of floor. Have a go at sliding back and forth. You can make this into an almost Olympic game by measuring how far you can travel in a single slide. Try having a competition with a friend or family member to see who can slide the furthest.

# A MORE EXCITING DIARY

People keep diaries as a way of having a record of everything that happened to them that day. The problem with keeping a diary is that, most of the time, your day probably isn't all that exciting.

Start a diary, but instead of recording the things that actually happened to you, make up a more exciting day. One that's filled with all the fun, interesting, exhilarating things you would do if you could.

Thinking about all the most exciting things you could be doing is a good way of planning your life, ensuring that you're aware of all the things you like doing (and want more of in your life).

## TUESDAY

Dear Diary,

Today I had ice cream for breakfast. School was cancelled because of snow, so my best friend Celia came round and we went sledding. Then we went to the zoo and fed the parakeets before going to the cinema to watch a movie. My parents let us stay up late so we made a big midnight feast of crisps and chocolate and played video games. The best part was that my little brother wasn't allowed a turn.

# HALLWAY BOWLING

Bowling is a surprisingly old sport – indeed, it might be one of the oldest. Early versions of bowling were played by the ancient Egyptians over 7,000 years ago (archaeologists found a set of pins and a ball in a child's tomb).

You don't have to go to an alley to bowl; you can play using items you find around the house.

Find some plastic bottles and a ball. Set up the bottles at one end of the hallway and stand with the ball at the other. Practise rolling the ball to knock over the bottles.

You can also play with a sibling or parent, keeping score with a pen and paper.

# KARL OR CHRISTMAS?

Karl Marx was a German philosopher and economist. He had long white hair and a big bushy white beard – rather like Father Christmas, in fact.

See if you can spot Father Christmas hiding among all the Karl Marxes.

# HOME OLYMPICS

The Olympic Games are held every four years. They have been going for a very long time; the first ones were held in ancient Greece more than 2,500 years ago. They involve lots of different games or events participated in by all the major countries of the world.

Turn your home into an Olympic stadium. All the inhabitants become 'athletes'. The goal is to set a variety of challenges and add up the points that are accumulated in each round. 'Games' might include:

- A speed contest for running six times around the kitchen table.
- A hallway egg and spoon race.
- A push-up contest.
- A breath-holding contest.
- A sitting still contest.

Hand out trophies and medals for the winners – you can make these out of paper.

# DEFEAT THE PEN OR PENCIL

There are around 14 billion pens and another 15 billion pencils made each year across the world. Most of them never get used fully – they tend to get lost or broken before all the lead or ink has been used up.

Find an old pen or pencil. Set yourself the mission of using it all up in one afternoon, either wearing it down to the ferrule (that's the little metal bit at the end of a pencil) or using up all the ink.

Do this however you like, drawing lines, circles or other shapes, writing pages and pages of nonsense, or just scribbling all over the paper. When you're finished you'll be left either with an entirely clear pen or a tiny stub of a pencil – both of which are very rare (and satisfying) trophies.

# FILTHY TONGUES

Here is a collection of some words in languages from around the world. All of them are quite rude:

→ *Ta gueule* (French)
→ *Culo* (Italian)
→ *Unchi* (うんち) (Japanese)
→ *Peido* (Portuguese)
→ *Debil* (дебил) (Russian)
→ *Bèn dàn* (笨蛋) (Chinese)
→ *Hirnlose Ochse* (German)
→ *Kusi* (Finnish)

Without using your phone, try to find the translations of as many of them as you can. Look them up in foreign language dictionaries (you can find these in your library) or see if there's an adult who can help you. Alternately, have a guess as to what each of them might mean.

| WORD: | MEANING? |
|---|---|
| 🇫🇷 *Ta gueule* | |
| 🇮🇹 *Culo* | |
| 🇯🇵 *Unchi* (うんち) | |
| *Peido* | |
| *Debil* (дебил) | |
| *Bèn dàn* (笨蛋) | |
| *Hirnlose Ochse* | |
| 🇫🇮 *Kusi* | |

# COUNT YOUR BLESSINGS

It's easy to forget just how many good things there are in your life. So why not try counting them? Get a pen and paper and make a list of all the good things you have in your life.

In my life, I have:

\_\_\_\_ people who love me

\_\_\_\_ friends at school

\_\_\_\_ toys I like to play with

\_\_\_\_ TV shows I like watching

\_\_\_\_ nice memories of things that have happened to me

\_\_\_\_ places I like visiting

\_\_\_\_ different meals that I enjoy eating

\_\_\_\_ exciting things I'm looking forward to in the next year.

If you can think of more good things to count, keep going. Try to make the list as long as possible.

When you've finished, it's a wise idea to keep the list somewhere close by. When you're feeling sad, stressed or upset, it can be a way of reminding yourself just how many blessings you have in your life.

# SPOT THE DIFFERENCE IN THE SNOW

This is a very famous painting called *The Hunters in the Snow* by the artist Pieter Brueghel.

We've made five small changes to the version on the right.
See how many you can spot.

# MAKE YOURSELF TINY GAME

It's probably been a while since you were very small, but trying to fold yourself into the smallest possible space is still pretty fun, especially if you can hang out in the tiny space for a while.

Try to find some of the smallest hiding places in the house. It could be the space between the washing machine and the back wall, or the frame of the kitchen window.

Squeeze yourself into the tiny space and see how long you can last.

Play this game with someone either bigger or smaller than you: marvel at how much better you are at this – or at the advantages they have over you.

 If you're having trouble fitting, or if the space is filled with things that look as if they might be a bit dangerous, like cables, it's safer to look for somewhere else.

# PUTTING THINGS IN ORDER

There is something strangely pleasurable about putting things in order. So much of life lies outside of our control – whether it will be nice enough to play outside, whether our parents will be in a good enough mood to drive us over to a friend's house – that when there's a part of it that we can govern and bring order to, we feel a sense of pride and calm.

Find a place in your home that's in a bit of a jumble, and bring some much-needed order to bear. You might try:

→ Arranging the books on your bookshelves into alphabetical order (or by colour).

→ Sorting the shoes by the door in order of size (smallest to largest).

→ Organising the contents of the kitchen cupboards into categories (all the jars on the left, all the packets in the middle, all the cans on the right).

→ Stacking all the pans in the kitchen drawers properly (largest on the bottom, smallest on the top).

→ Arranging all the cushions on the sofa neatly.

Ask your parents if there is anything around the house you can bring order to.

They will probably be extremely grateful for your efforts!

# DONALD'S SQUIGGLE GAME

Donald Winnicott was a psychologist who did most of his work with children. He wasn't at all stuffy or dull: in fact, he believed that playing and using your imagination was one of the most important and valuable things children could do. He invented a drawing game he called the 'squiggle' game, which we've included below.

Turn the squiggles on the page below into drawings, incorporating the squiggle into the design. Think about what the shape of the squiggle suggests to you. Might one of them look like a mouth? Or the brim of a hat? Or an elephant's trunk? Try to go with your very first spontaneous impression.

# PHILOSOPHICAL QUESTIONS

A philosophical question is a question about a very big idea – like reality, or God, or the meaning of life – that doesn't have an obvious answer. Many clever people have spent their entire lives trying to answer particular philosophical questions.

We've included some philosophical questions below to get you started. See what answers you can come up with, and ask the same questions to other people to see what they think.

→ Dreams feel just like real life – until you wake up, that is. So how do you know that you're not dreaming now?

→ We know that thinking takes place in the brain. But what are thoughts actually made of? Could you look at a thought under a microscope?

→ Objects tend to have a purpose. The purpose of a hammer is to hit nails. The purpose of scissors is to cut paper. The purpose of a chair is to support a sitting person. Do you think humans have a purpose? What might that purpose be?

→ Is it ever okay to steal? What if you were very poor? Would it be okay to steal food to feed your family? Where should the line be drawn?

→ Can you think of an occasion where the 'right' thing to do would be to lie rather than tell the truth?

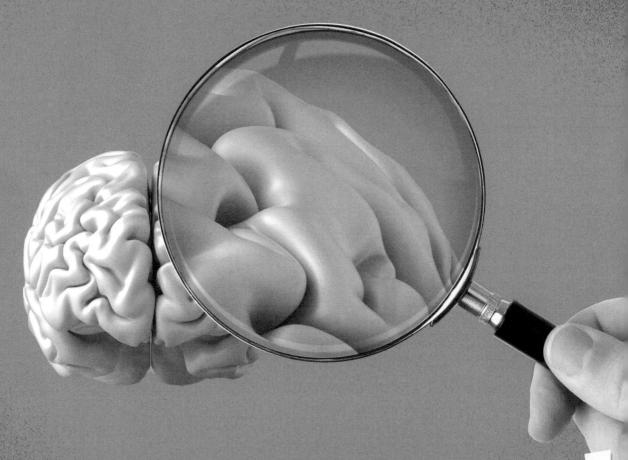

# RE-STAINED GLASS WINDOWS

You'll often find stained-glass windows in old churches. These are made up of lots of small pieces of coloured glass, usually depicting characters and scenes from the Bible. Often they're very beautiful indeed.

Here's an example from the Notre-Dame Cathedral in Paris.

We've removed all the colours. Add them back in using whatever colours you like.

# THE ULTIMATE APOLOGY

When people do something very wrong, they're sometimes asked to write a 'letter of apology'. Maybe you've once had to write one of those – for being mean to or annoying someone. Imagine you've done something very bad, and you have to write a letter of apology. How might such a letter go in the following cases:

→ You've lost the school hamster when looking after it overnight and have to say sorry to the whole class.

→ You've done a very loud fart during an important speech by the president.

→ You've accidentally kicked a football through your headmaster's window.

→ You've lost your nation's Olympic team kit shortly before the start of the games, meaning they'll have to wear only their underwear to the opening ceremony.

→ You've drawn whiskers on your neighbour's baby.

Try to sound extremely apologetic as you explain, in detail, what you did and why.

# THE BOOK OF SILLINESS

Even though most people keep this very hidden, everyone has done a lot of silly things in their life, even people who look pretty serious and competent. Maybe they forgot their own name at an important party or spilt a drink down the front of their boss...

It's very important to know the silliest things that people around you have done, because it will make you feel less bad about silly things that you end up doing.

Get hold of a cheap exercise book and title it THE BOOK OF SILLINESS. Go around a selection of adults and some other children too and ask them to tell you the silliest, dumbest, maddest things they have ever done.
Give each person a fresh page.

When you're feeling down and are sure you're the only nincompoop in town, look up your precious book: it might just save your life!

# FILL IN THE BLANKS

To the right, we've written the opening of a story, with some crucial details left out. Fill them in to make the story your own. Use your imagination to make them as wild as you like!

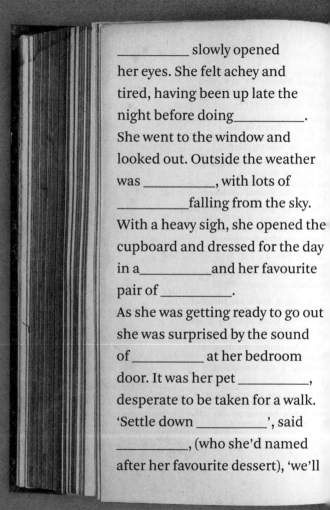

_____ slowly opened her eyes. She felt achey and tired, having been up late the night before doing_____. She went to the window and looked out. Outside the weather was _____, with lots of _____falling from the sky. With a heavy sigh, she opened the cupboard and dressed for the day in a_____and her favourite pair of _____.

As she was getting ready to go out she was surprised by the sound of _____ at her bedroom door. It was her pet _____, desperate to be taken for a walk. 'Settle down _____', said _____, (who she'd named after her favourite dessert), 'we'll

be out in a minute.'
After putting on the leash, they headed downstairs together. Just as she was opening the door, _____ noticed a letter lying on the mat. It was addressed to her in unfamiliar handwriting. She picked it up and opened it.

'Dear _____,' it read, 'I'm writing to you in a time of great need. As an expert in _____ your services are required to help _____ the lost _____, which we suspect has been stolen by the forces of _____.'
Yours faithfully,
_____

'I hope you're ready for a long walk _____' she said, tugging on the leash. 'We've got a job to do.'

If you're feeling inspired, keep going, writing the next part of the story on your own.

# A CONVERSATION MENU

Most menus sit in the middle of the table in restaurants and have suggestions about what people might want to eat. Design another kind of menu, a 'Conversation Menu', that tells people what they should talk about during a meal. Here is one we've designed:

Now design your own...

CONVERSATION MENU

### STARTERS
Who is your favourite teacher and why?
What are the different sorts of sounds your farts make?
What makes someone a good friend?

### MAINS
Would you rather live to be 100 but only be a bit happy or live to 40 and be very happy everyday?
What animal do you think is most like you and why?
What are you afraid people might laugh about you for?

### DESSERTS
Who deserves to be rich and who doesn't?
Describe your ideal hotel.
What period of history would you like to be able to go back and visit?

# DESIGN YOUR OWN PIRATE FLAG

Pirates are sea-faring robbers who steal valuable cargo from other ships. In the 18th century, when piracy was at its height, famous pirates like Edward Teach ('Blackbeard') or Bartholomew Roberts ('Black Bart') would sail the seas looking for trading ships to burgle. They would fly their own unique pirate flag as a way of letting these ships know they were about to be boarded (and scaring them into co-operating). The most famous example is the Jolly Roger or 'Skull and Crossbones' flag, but other pirates made their own designs.

Design your own pirate flag using paper and colouring pencils. Make the design as terrifying as possible using dark colours and symbols of death (skulls, devils, weapons or monsters) or of anything else that you think might scare people. You can then 'fly' the flag by putting it up on your bedroom door as a warning to anyone who might want to come in.

# HAUNT YOUR OWN HOUSE

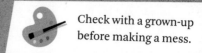

Check with a grown-up before making a mess.

Nowadays most people don't believe in ghosts unless they're very superstitious (or watch too many programmes about psychics and haunted houses on television). That makes it fun to pretend to be one.

Dress up like a ghost. An old bedsheet with some eyeholes cut out will do (ask your parents for one you could use). You might try to add some accessories – like some bloodstains (made from ketchup), or some clanking chains (made from a metal dog leash or some old jewellery). If you're lucky you might have a Halloween costume you could use.

Next, try haunting your own house with some classic ghostly manoeuvres:

→ Moaning and groaning.
→ Moving objects or furniture when no one is looking.
→ Following other people without being seen.
→ Tapping on doors and walls.
→ Rattling chains.
→ Whispering 'curses' on family members.

The standard way to get rid of a ghost is to 'release' them by following a request they've made, like saying a blessing, or giving them a proper memorial. If your family are getting tired of your ghostly antics, simply set them a task that will put your soul at rest.

# MAPS OF IMAGINARY PLACES

Maps are a guide to the terrain of a place – usually a particular country, or of the entire world. Not all of them are accurate. Some very old maps made before the whole world had been explored included islands that didn't exist or imaginary details (like monsters). Other maps have been made for places that only exist in someone's imagination – like in fantasy novels.

Draw a map of an imaginary country. Fill it with all the things you'd find on a map of regular places – roads, hills, rivers, lakes, mountains, villages, towns and cities. You can use an existing map for reference.

Use your imagination to complete the details. What is the terrain like? What are all the different cities called? Are there monsters?

CITYVILLE

JAGGED MOUNTAINS

LOCAL
DRAGON

WOBBLY
BRIDGE

BUMPY HILLS

# OUTDOOR ARTWORKS

We often think that 'art' is just another word for 'painting' or 'drawing'. But works of art can be made out of all sorts of different things. 'Found' artworks are made not from paint or pencils, but from objects the artist has found in the outside world.

If you're out in the park, or in the garden, try to make a work of art out of the things you find lying on the ground – like fallen leaves, or rocks, or grass clippings.

Can you make:
A circle out of leaves?
A tower out of pebbles?
A star shape out of twigs?

# ANSWERS

*Ta gueule* – Shut your mouth
*Culo* – Bum
*Unchi* うんち – Poop
*Peido* – Fart
*Debil* (дебил) – Moron
*Bèn dàn (笨蛋)* – Fool
*Hirnlose Ochse* – Mindless ox
*Husi* – Pee

(+/-) 14 + 13 - 56 + 100 - 18 = 53
(x/÷) 2 x 8 ÷ 16 x 3 x 10 = 30
(+/-) 77 - 12 + 1 - 11 + 6 = 61
(x /÷) 101 x 8 x 3 ÷ 4 x 11 = 6666

Philosophers'
Wordsearch,
p.103 →

Filthy Tongues,
p.114 ←

Spot the
Difference in
the Snow,
p. 118 →

Summing
It Up, p.102 ←

| D | E | B | E | A | U | V | O | I | R |
|---|---|---|---|---|---|---|---|---|---|
| I | E | W | K | B | K | Z | L | R | O |
| D | J | S | O | C | R | A | T | E | S |
| E | I | A | C | M | L | H | U | M | E |
| R | S | R | Y | A | V | G | C | R | R |
| O | K | T | D | R | R | A | W | L | S |
| T | J | R | V | X | Q | T | Q | H | Q |
| O | H | E | G | E | L | X | E | B | I |
| X | Y | T | J | C | A | M | U | S | M |
| G | P | N | F | P | A | S | C | A | L |

# IMAGES

## Indoor Entomology
Paul Taylor / Stone / Getty Images
Science Photo Library / Getty Images
Nastasic / DigitalVision Vectors / Getty Images
Mikroman6 / Moment / Getty Images
Ilka & Franz / DigitalVision / Getty Images
PM Images / DigitalVision / Getty Images
Mary Orvis Marbury / Raw Pixel
Charles Dessalines D' Orbigny / Raw Pixel
Anselmus Boëtius de Boodt / Raw Pixel
Irin-k / Shutterstock

## Knight-in-Dining-Armour
CSA Images / Getty Images
Colin Anderson Productions pty ltd / Stone / Getty Images
Wong Sze Fei / EyeEm / Getty Images
Poh Kim Yeoh / EyeEm / Getty Images
AlenKadr / Shutterstock
Studioloco / Shutterstock
Ivan Kurmyshov / Shutterstock
Rustle / Shutterstock
Shawn Hempel / Shutterstock

## Not-so-super-heroes
AntonMaltsev / Shutterstock
BCFC / Shutterstock
Bergamont / Shutterstock
SeDmi / Shutterstock
Aprilphoto / Shutterstock
COLOA Studio / Shutterstock
Azure1 / Shutterstock
SOMMAI / Shutterstock
Ines Behrens-Kunkel / Shutterstock
StunningArt / Shutterstock

## Window Stakeout
CSA Images / Vetta / Getty Images
Morgan Housel / Unsplash
Jerry Marks Productions / UpperCut Images / Getty Images

Hill Creek Pictures / UpperCut Images / Getty Images
Rubberball / Nicole Hill Getty Images
FotoVoyager / E+ / Getty Images
Gandee Vasan / Stone / Getty Images
Alan Tunnicliffe Photography / Moment / Getty Images
WIN-Initiative / Stone / Getty Images
KOLOstock / DigitalVision / Getty Images
Andrei Puzakov / EyeEm / Getty Images
Kunchit Jantana / EyeEm / Getty Images
Ljupco Smokovski / Shutterstock
Eric Isselee / Shutterstock
FangXiaNuo / E+ / Getty Images
Jay Reilly / UpperCut Images / Getty Images

## Poo Eulogy
Natalia Dobryanskaya / Shutterstock
Kzenon / Shutterstock
New Africa / Shutterstock
Ekaterina43 / Shutterstock
Len4foto / Shutterstock
Charnsitr / Shutterstock

## My Utopia
Valery Sidelnykov / Shutterstock
LuFeeTheBear / Shutterstock
PavelShynkarou / Shutterstock

## Still Life
Paul Cézanne, The Basket of Apples, c. 1893. Oil on canvas, 65 cm × 80 cm. Art Institute of Chicago, Chicago, USA / Raw Pixel
Paul Gauguin, Wood Tankard and Metal Pitcher, 1880. Oil on canvas, 54 × 65 cm. Art Institute of Chicago, Chicago, USA / Raw Pixel
TR STOK / Shutterstock
Ffolas / Shutterstock
Sergio Foto / Shutterstock

## Impress Your Parents
S-F / Shutterstock

**Rude Words**
Mega Pixel / Shutterstock

**Newstaches**
Rtimages / Shutterstock
Mimagephotography / Shutterstock
Mega Pixel / Shutterstock
Wmaireche / Shutterstock
Minerva Studio / Shutterstock

**Feckless Necklace**
Winai Tepsuttinun / Shutterstock
PIXbank CZ / Shutterstock
ANTONIO TRUZZI / Shutterstock
AtSkwongPhoto / Shutterstock
Lehun / Shutterstock
Agsaz / Shutterstock
Eyepark / Shutterstock

**Racing Raindrops**
Mega Pixel / Shutterstock

**Interview Your Grandmother**
Ollyy / Shutterstock
Zieusin / Shutterstock

**Paint Like Picasso**
Africa Studio / Shutterstock
Pablo Picasso, Woman in a Green Hat, 1947. Oil on canvas, Albertina Museum, Vienna, Austria. Adam Ján Figel / Alamy Stock Photo © Succession Picasso / DACS, London 2021
Pablo Picasso, Still Life with a Mandolin, 1924. Oil on canvas, 101 x 158 cm. National Gallery of Ireland, Dublin, Ireland. Bequeathed, Máire MacNeill Sweeney, 1987. agefotostock / Alamy Stock Photo © Succession Picasso / DACS, London 2021

**Bottle Instrument**
Dwphotos / Shutterstock
Inga Nielsen / Shutterstock
Nerthuz / Shutterstock
Sraphotohut / Shutterstock
Pashkovska Tetyana / Shutterstock

**Meditation**
L-house / Shutterstock
Halfmax.ru / Shutterstock

**Andrey tiyk** / Shutterstock
Yanik88 / Shutterstock
Ninja SS / Shutterstock
Alexander Baluev / Shutterstock

**Steering Blind**
James.Pintar / Shutterstock
Andrew Angelov / Shutterstock
Kamira777 / Shutterstock
Gerasimov_foto_174 / Shutterstock
Roam Free Photography / Shutterstock

**Good News**
Rtimages / Shutterstock
Castleski / Shutterstock
Jo Panuwat D / Shutterstock

**Change Your View**
Rose Carson / Shutterstock
Nexus 7 / Shutterstock
Solarseven / Shutterstock
Dima Zel / Shutterstock
AmeliAU / Shutterstock
Ktsdesign / Shutterstock

**Cut-Up Technique**
Wacpan / Shutterstock

**Cleaning Pioneer**
Ljupco Smokovski / Shutterstock
Valentin Valkov / Shutterstock
Kittyfly / Shutterstock

**Becoming an Animal**
Eric Isselee / Shutterstock

**Cloud Watching**
Phloxii / Shutterstock
Suzanne Tucker / Shutterstock

**Bored Stiff**
Peter Porrini / Shutterstock

**Your Own Orchard**
Stockphoto-graf / Shutterstock
Vaclav Volrab / Shutterstock
MR.ANUWAT / Shutterstock
Arka38 / Shutterstock
Bozena Fulawka / Shutterstock

**Combining Flavours**
Pathdoc / Shutterstock
Kiselev Andrey Valerevich / Shutterstock
Nicoleta Ionescu / Shutterstock
Medvid.com / Shutterstock

**Life Predictions**
Monkey Business Images / Shutterstock
AboutLife / Shutterstock

**Leaf Pressing**
CoffeeChocolates / Shutterstock
Vladimir Sukhachev / Shutterstock

**Unique Perspectives**
Artazum / Shutterstock

**Concocting Constellations**
Ollyy / Shutterstock
Skylines / Shutterstock

**Memory Capsule**
Sergiy Bykhunenko / Shutterstock
Photastic / Shutterstock
Aleksandar Mijatovic / Shutterstock
Onk-Q / Shutterstock
Kobkob / Shutterstock
Christin Lola / Shutterstock
Rido / Shutterstock

**Poememory**
Mega Pixel / Shutterstock

**Receipt Top Trumps**
Hue Ta / Shutterstock

**Surprising Enterprise**
AleksandrN / Shutterstock
Susan Schmitz / Shutterstock

**Body Knowledge**
Tetiana Rostopira / Shutterstock

**Penny Finders**
John Gomez / Shutterstock

**Feed the Birds**
Luis Louro / Shutterstock
Picsfive / Shutterstock
CoffeeChocolates / Shutterstock
Robert Chao / Shutterstock
Sergey Uryadnikov / Shutterstock

**New Gods**
Pxl.store / Shutterstock
Zwiebackesser / Shutterstock

**Stand and Deliver**
2xSamara.com / Shutterstock
Ammeepinko / Shutterstock
Gowithstock / Shutterstock
UMBE / Shutterstock
Asier Romero / Shutterstock
Andrey_Kuzmin / Shutterstock
Altin Osmanaj / Shutterstock

**Egg Family**
Palo_ok / Shutterstock

**Dressing Up, Up and Up**
Sabphoto / Shutterstock
Pencil case / Shutterstock

**Precious Suitcase**
Sirtravelalot / Shutterstock

**Drawpreciation**
Spacezerocom / Shutterstock
Antonio Guillem / Shutterstock
Peter Titmuss / Shutterstock

**Recipe for Disaster**
Romix Image / Shutterstock

**My Chimera**
Eric Isselee / Shutterstock

**Grue-seum**
Blackboard1965 / Shutterstock
ZONAGIALLA / Shutterstock
Autsawin uttisin / Shutterstock
Olga Popova / Shutterstock
SimoneN / Shutterstock
Mega Pixel / Shutterstock

**New Words**
Sergey Goryachev / Shutterstock
Jet Cat Studio / Shutterstock

**Back to Front**
A2bb5s / Shutterstock
Gelpi / Shutterstock

**The Story of an Object**
Pcruciatti / Shutterstock
Paul Michael Hughes / Shutterstock
E-ART / Shutterstock
Mega Pixel / Shutterstock
Squeeb Creative / Shutterstock
New Africa / Shutterstock

**Taste Tester**
Donatas1205 / Shutterstock
Onair / Shutterstock

**Summing it up**
Vectorfusionart / Shutterstock

**Vow of Silence**
Warut Chinsai / Shutterstock

**Sock Sliding**
New Africa / Shutterstock

**A More Exciting Diary**
Antonio Gravante / Shutterstock
M. Unal Ozmen / Shutterstock
Binimin / Shutterstock
Oksana Shufrych / Shutterstock

**Hallway Bowling**
Boris Medvedev / Shutterstock
Abd / Shutterstock
Stockphoto-graf / Shutterstock
Pond Saksit / Shutterstock
Mindscape studio / Shutterstock

**Karl or Christmas?**
Kiselev Andrey Valerevich / Shutterstock
Severjn / Shutterstock

Everett Collection / Shutterstock

**Home Olympics**
PaulPaladin / Shutterstock

**Defeat the Pen or Pencil**
Gavran333 / Shutterstock

**Filthy Tongues**
Rawpixel.com / Shutterstock
Lana2016 / Shutterstock

**Count Your Blessings**
A Lot Of People / Shutterstock

**Spot the Difference in the Snow**
Pieter Brueghel the Elder, The Hunters in the Snow, 1565. Oil on panel, 117 × 162 cm. Kunsthistorisches Museum, Vienna, Austria / Kunsthistorisches Museum / DeAgostini / G. NIMATALLAH / Getty Images

**Donald's Squiggle Game**
Puttography / Shutterstock

**Philosophical Questions**
Dinga / Shutterstock
R.classen / Shutterstock

**Re-strained Glass Windows**
Snowyns / Shutterstock
Dmitry Naumov / Shutterstock
Aquila / Shutterstock
Bruce Bennett / Getty Images

**The Ultimate Apology**
Olesya Zhuk / Shutterstock

**Fill in the Blanks**
Boumen Japet / Shutterstock
Scisetti Alfio / Shutterstock

**Design Your Own Pirate Flag**
RG-vc / Shutterstock

**Haunt Your Own House**
FOTOKITA / Shutterstock
Sergey Spritnyuk / Shutterstock
Andrey_Popov / Shutterstock

**Maps of Imaginary Places**
MIGUEL G. SAAVEDRA / Shutterstock
Alex Staroseltsev / Shutterstock

**Outdoor Artworks**
Gita Kulinitch Studio / Shutterstock

**Cover**
Chones / Shutterstock
Pick / Shutterstock
Mega Pixel / Shutterstock
Chones / Shutterstock
Paul Taylor / Stone / Getty Images
Pongsakorn chaina / Shutterstock
Mary Orvis Marbury / Raw Pixel

The School of Life is a global organisation helping people lead more fulfilled lives. It is a resource for helping us understand ourselves, for improving our relationships, our careers and our social lives – as well as for helping us find calm and get more out of our leisure hours. We do this through films, workshops, books, apps, gifts and community. You can find us online, in stores and in welcoming spaces around the globe.

THESCHOOLOFLIFE.COM